Klay Thompson: The Inspiring Story of One of Basketball's Sharpest Shooters

An Unauthorized Biography

By: Clayton Geoffreys

Table of Contents

Foreword

It should not be much of a surprise that Klay Thompson made it in the NBA. A former high school standout and star at Washington State, Klay has always been a deadly threat on the basketball court. Alongside superstar Stephen Curry, the two have formed the Splash Brothers, a dynamic duo that rains threes from outside the arc on a nightly basis. As of the 2014-2015 NBA season, Klay Thompson shoots an impressive career 41% from three-point land. Fresh off signing a four-year, $70 million contract with the Golden State Warriors, Klay has a promising career ahead of him. The Bay Area has also begun to rumble as the Warriors have emerged a premier team in the West under the leadership of rookie coach Steve Kerr. Thank you for downloading *Klay Thompson: The Incredible Story of One of Basketball's Sharpest Shooters*. In this unauthorized biography, we will learn Klay's incredible life story and impact on the game of basketball. Hope you enjoy and if you do, please do not forget to leave a review!

Also, check out my website at claytongeoffreys.com to join my exclusive list where I let you know about my latest books and give you goodies!

Cheers,

Clayton Geoffreys

Visit me at <u>www.claytongeoffreys.com</u>

Introduction

When it comes to the ability to shoot three-pointers, there are few players who have perfected that skill better than Klay Thompson. Klay was born with the pedigree of an NBA player and a shooting stroke that can be compared to that of former NBA players like Reggie Miller and Alan Houston. Thompson's genetic makeup has also helped him in his ability to play multiple sports, such as baseball and football, though basketball has always remained his top sport.

Klay grew up in Oregon, mainly because his father used to play for, and was drafted by, the Portland Trailblazers. Klay did not have to undergo the dramatic, difficult upbringings that most other rags-to-riches athletes were subjected to in their lives. Unlike some other NBA stars, he was not raised in a neighborhood ravaged by crime or gang wars. He always had food on the table, and his family was always there to provide and support for him, sometimes even more than what he needed. He lived a comfortable life and had a father who was always present for the family. Just because Klay was born with a silver spoon in his mouth though, does not mean that his road to the NBA was as easy as you might imagine.

Growing up with father Mychal Thompson, who was a 2-time NBA Champion and a former top overall draft pick, was indeed beneficial and fruitful for Klay Thompson and his brothers. His father instilled in him and his siblings the qualities and the proper mentality needed to play as a professional athlete. His father's stories and his own natural curiosity made Klay more and more determined to become a professional basketball player in the NBA.

After completing high school, he found himself in a tough position. He had to choose where he was going to take his talents now that he'd be playing at the collegiate level. Ever since he was a little kid shooting jumpers, he had always dreamed of playing in the Pac

10. Although he didn't receive many offers from Pac-10 schools, one university decided to take a chance on the kid: Washington State. Playing for the Washington State Cougars ignited Klay's fire to continue to improve over the following years. Pegged as a one-way shooter, Klay took it upon himself to get better on the offensive end, but more importantly, on the defensive end.

He was always overlooked when playing basketball, never given the credit he deserved, yet Klay continued to press on. His father played a major role in teaching him valuable life lessons that helped to keep him grounded. Klay played three remarkable years at the college level. However, he failed to make it to the NCAA tournament. Although many skeptics suggested that he was never given the supporting cast he needed to take the Cougars to the next level, many still believe that a player's legacy is based on team wins, not just individual performances.

In 2011, the Golden State Warriors drafted Klay with the 11th pick. As destiny would have it, Klay and his father were connected through Jerry West. West was responsible for trading for Mychal Thompson back in the day when he was drafted 1st overall by the Portland Trailblazers. You could say that Jerry West struck gold twice by having these two Thompsons on his two different franchise teams.

In the 2011 NBA Draft, the Warriors decided to take their chances with Klay. Even though they were lacking a big man presence, and even though they already had Monta Ellis as their main shooting guard, they were so invested in Klay's high upside that it did not matter to them that they were not drafting a big player. Klay had to prove himself in the NBA as a two-way shooting guard, which is arguably a dying breed in the NBA. There aren't many shooting guards (or players, for that matter) who play both ends of the floor with the same intensity.

After being chosen by the Warriors, many rumors surfaced about Monta Ellis being moved. After dismissing the rumors of Ellis being traded, Klay tried his best to produce off the bench, or play the small forward position. Slowly but surely Ellis was traded for Aussie big man Andrew Bogut. This was a much-anticipated move for Golden State, as they really needed some inside presence. Although Bogut's history of injury may have raised questions about the risk the Warriors took, it eventually paid off as Klay was given more minutes to play and immediately became the team's main shooting guard.

After becoming Golden State's starting two-guard, Klay quickly became one of the best up and coming shooters in the league. Unlike other three-point threats who mainly camped outside to stretch the floor or for catch-and-shoot situations, Thompson was a volume shooter who could also become the Warriors' go-to-guy at any given moment. As such, he also developed into a great scorer and arguably one of the best shooters around. Those qualities were what made Klay an All-Star and one of the most productive players during the Golden State Warrior's championship run in 2015.

With hard work and dedication, Klay has become one of the key pieces in a championship Golden State Warriors team. He is the second offensive option for the Warriors and is arguably the best shooter not named Stephen Curry. Klay's efforts earned him an All-Star appearance as well as an All-NBA Third Team selection. What seems most memorable about Klay Thompson was when he exploded in a third quarter with an NBA record of 37 points. When Klay gets hot, his shooting stroke is automatic and he suddenly becomes one of the deadliest shooters in the NBA. Talk about microwave!

Klay and point guard Stephen Curry, who is also the son of an ex-NBA player, Dell Curry, formed a terrific combination. These two sharpshooters were quickly becoming one of the best backcourt combinations in the NBA. They terrorized their opponents with their shooting ability and could shoot lights out on any given night. Fans affectionately called the backcourt duo the "Splash Brothers." To this day, Curry and Thompson are arguably the best backcourt in the NBA and have been the main catalysts for ending their team's 40-year championship drought.

Chapter 1: Childhood and Early Life

Klay Alexander Thompson was born on February 8th, 1990 in Los Angeles, California. He is the son of Mychal Sr. and Julie, and brother to Mychel, who would also become a very good basketball player, and Trayce, who would go on to play professional baseball. His father, Mychal Thompson, is of Bohemian descent, and was drafted 1st overall in the 1978 draft by the Portland Trailblazers. After playing 14 seasons in the NBA, most notably with the Los Angeles Lakers, he managed to help the Lakers franchise win two championships in the late 80's, playing alongside Magic Johnson and Kareem Abdul-Jabbar. As you can imagine, these are some big shoes to fill. The Thompson family proved to have good athletic genes, because Julie was also a good volleyball player who played in the Division 1 level during her college years.[i] Klay is the middle child of the three and is often described as being less outgoing and more of the quiet and inquisitive type. He was always excited about each opportunity he had to learn and often asked a barrage of questions whenever something sparked his interest. Mychal and Julie always worried where Klay might be as he would often disappear to a corner and read his books. Mychal quickly realized that Klay's personality was an offshoot from his mother. Klay and his two brothers lived the majority of their childhood south of Portland, in Lake Oswego.

They grew up and lived there until Klay's 8th grade year, but it was in Lake Oswego where the fate of two future NBA All-Stars aligned. As fate may have it, Klay was on the very same little league baseball team as Kevin Love. They dominated with their impressive skills and managed to win a state title and were just a few games short of the Little League World Series. Klay was a dedicated baseball player who could play every position on the field with the exception of catcher. Kevin Love, on the other hand, was on the pitching mound standing at a gigantic 6'1 stature during the 5th grade. Talk about intimidating! How often do you see someone in the fifth grade at that height trying to whip a baseball down the mound? The two would later on choose to play basketball, each for their own different reasons. As early as the 2nd grade though, Klay and Love were already playing one-on-one basketball.[ii]

It was around the same time that battles in the backyard began with the Thompson family. Klay never had the chance to tag along with his dad to his basketball practices as a young child, unlike his older brother Mychel. Mychal had already been out of the league before Klay turned 2 and spent the rest of his years working as a broadcast analyst for the Lakers. His earliest recollections of basketball were during his playing days in CYO Rec. Mychal always caught his son Klay playing in the back imagining himself as Penny, Kobe, or Allan Houston.

There were 4 males in the family, so epic 2-on-2 games were consistently played. This all began when

Mychal Thompson decided to hang a basketball net in the backyard of their family's home. The teams always consisted of two-time NBA Champion Mychal Thompson and his youngest son Trayce against his oldest son Mychel, who also plays professional basketball, and the middle son Klay.

It was in the backyard where the Thompsons developed their competitive edge. Klay and Mychel often accused their dad of cheating in order to let their youngest brother win. The games usually ended up with someone leaving in a huff and often got very intense due to the competitive nature of the Thompsons. Although the games were as competitive as can be, it was here where the training sessions started. Mychal was the one teaching them valuable lessons on the court and, as you can imagine, it really helped his kids understand the game of basketball at a whole new level. It's always a rare gem to have a father who used to play in the NBA.

Being the sons of a two-time NBA Champion can be pretty daunting at times. Klay and his brothers looked up to their dad and always took his advice to heart. All three brothers are currently pursuing their professional careers. Though Mychal provided the best advice to his sons, he was also their toughest critic and would scold them for anything they did incorrectly in their respective athletic endeavors. The same remains true even to this day.

Before Klay went to high school and at the age of 14, the family decided to move to Los Angeles where Mychal played during 12 seasons. Klay would go on to attend Santa Margarita Catholic High School and became a standout in his four years of play there.

Chapter 2: High School Years

Klay Thompson attended Santa Margarita Catholic High School where he quickly became one of the best young players in the country. As a freshman, Klay had a lot of interest in life outside of basketball. He was very fond of playing chess as a child and continues to play casually, even up to this day. However, he was a high school athlete and the pressures of society made him decide to avoid playing chess competitively.[iii] His high school coach also said that the young shooter was very fond of playing videogames. Klay was also a multi-purpose athlete. He played as a quarterback for his high school football team and reprised his love for baseball, his first sport, by playing as a pitcher. He knew he belonged on the hardwood floor above any other sport, though.

However good of an athlete Klay Thompson was in high school, and despite how good of a basketball player he is currently, his coach never thought that he would become a very good player in his early years in high school, despite having the genes of a former NBA player. High school coach Jerry DeBusk knew that Klay was a good player, but did not think that he could become a college-level athlete, much less a professional in the NBA.[iv] With that, Klay would mostly play as a role player in his first year of high school.

Santa Margarita was also a hotbed for Division I recruits, and Klay had to play behind older and better teammates. His brother Mychel had also played and starred for the same school several years before. With the amount of sheer talent on the team, Klay Thompson was very underrated and unheralded for his first few years of high school.

Much like during his freshman season, he remained a role player in his sophomore year. He was restricted to the role of sixth or seventh man and his purpose was to come into games specifically to shoot three-pointers. One of his best memories as a sophomore was his meeting in the CIF-Southern Section Division III-AA final with fellow future NBA star James Harden. Harden was older and much more skilled than Thompson was. Harden's Artesia beat Thompson's Santa Margarita in a 74-44 beat down. Klay knew, even back then, that Harden would become a star in the NBA and he wanted to become as good as he was, if not better.

Klay Thompson recounts that day when he lost to James Harden as one of the biggest turning points of his high school career. He knew that he had to work harder on his game. Klay Thompson quit playing on the football and baseball teams to work on his basketball skills. He had to get a shooting coach to improve his shooting form. That part of his game became his biggest weapon and remains so to this day.[v] Klay then started playing for a top AAU program, the SoCal All-Stars. However, he was just not good enough yet and was delegated to the 16 and under team, who had no other future NBA players aside from

Klay. In the meantime, fellow future NBA players Kevin Love and Brandon Jennings headlined the SoCal All-Stars main team.

Coming into his third year, Klay began to shine as a basketball player especially with so many older players graduating. DeBusk saw how hard Thompson had worked on his game. After all, Klay was able to get some advice on work ethic from guys like Clyde Drexler and Rasheed Wallace while he was growing up as an ex-pro's son in Portland. DeBusk worked Klay hard, especially on the defensive end. He knew that the young shooter already had a deadly stroke but needed him to evolve on both ends of the court, especially on the defensive end, considering that Thompson was always a tall player, having grown to 6'5" over the interim break. Klay used to be slow in high school but developed his speed and lateral movement with the help of some drills.

Klay became one of the go-to-guys in his third year. He also became one of the biggest reasons Santa

Margarita reached the Division III State Championships in the 2006-07 season. In that year, Thompson earned All-Second Team honors.

As a senior however, he took his awards to another level after leading the team to a 30-5 record and a Division III State Championship appearance. He was no doubt the best player on his team and many college programs started trying to recruit him. The University of California Los Angeles recruited Klay strongly, and the young shooter wanted to that particular school because it was closer to home. Thompson also wanted to go to USC. However, UCLA and USC opted recruit Malcolm Lee and DeMar DeRozan, respectively. One other college program, Washington State, kept its eye on Klay. Tony Bennett, Washington's coach back then, was very interested in Thompson's development.

In the Division III State Championship game, Klay Thompson had one of the most memorable performances of any high school player in California. He set a state finals record with seven 3-point shots made and scored 37 points to win the title game for Santa Margarita. That game was arguably his best as a prep player.

As a senior, Klay Thompson averaged 21 points per game. He also managed to collect a lot of awards along the way, such as Division III State Player of the Year, League MVP, First Team All-Trinity League, Third-Team All-Orange County, First Team Best in the West, and EA Sports Second Team All-American honors. More importantly, it was during Klay's high school career that he found himself playing in a men's league every summer. This league was filled with big talent, including Josh Childress and former NFL player Tony Gonzalez. At a very young age, Klay was intrigued and eager to learn about life as a pro. He was surrounded by athletes living the life of a professional and wanted to know more about it. It was here that Klay found his determination to make it to the big leagues.

After his high school career, Klay Thompson was on his way to the University of Washington. Among all of the other programs that recruited him, he was most interested to play for Washington because of the way Tony Bennett recruited him. He loved how Bennett did not pressure him into being the best possible player he could be right away just because he was the son of a former NBA player.

Chapter 3: College Years at Washington State

After Klay's ever-so-successful high school career in Santa Margarita Catholic, he decided to take his talents to Washington State University. It was not the easiest choice for Klay, as he always dreamt of playing for other schools. Growing up, he always wanted to play for a Pac-10 team or any basketball program near home, particularly UCLA or USC, but didn't receive many offers from them. Many found it extremely odd that Klay was always flying under the radar and was often overlooked.

During his high school stint, Klay and his older brother hooked up with AAU Coach Joedy Gardner. It was during his time under Coach Gardner that Klay competed against future NBA players such as Aaron Afflalo, Tayshaun Prince, Kevin Love, and Tyson Chandler. His father held Coach Gardner in high regard and described him as one of the best shooting and technical coaches in the country. That just goes to show how much of an impact Gardner had on Klay's development. Klay was a humble and quiet kid and did not expect too many theatrics from his coach. Coach Gardner, however, decided to give him the full package. He taught Klay how to develop balance and arch by using a wide array of equipment. From towels to rubber bands and hula-hoops, all of these tools were used to help improve Klay's shooting ability.

Coach Gardner realized that he had found something special in Klay while teaching him how to become a better shooter, and he knew that a number of teams were going to be rushing to get him.

Enter Mike Burns, who served as an assistant to Tony Bennett, the Head Coach of the Washington State University Cougars in 2003-2004. As fate had it, Burns agreed on a summer stint with an elite AAU team that included Klay Thompson and Jrue Holiday. Burns later connected with Bennett while coaching Klay, and was perplexed by the fact that not many teams were attempting to recruit him. A lot of sports analysts claimed schools believed that Klay could not be defensive, but Burns quickly dismissed this notion. He claimed that Klay was the only player who was able to guard a specific player on the Atlanta Celtics team.

WSU was suddenly in the market for a wing player and they set their eyes on Klay. Bennett then contacted Gardner, who described Klay as a good prospect. It came down to three teams: WSU, Notre Dame, and Michigan. Gardner eventually had lunch with Klay to discuss basketball. Klay valued his coach so much that he needed his advice to decide on which school he should attend. A simple question had surfaced in which Klay asked Coach Gardner what he would do if he was in his situation. Gardner told him he would go to Washington State University, if it were up to him, and that's where Klay decided to go.

Freshman Season

In his freshman year at Washington State University, the 6'6" guard played in all 33 games in an impressive fashion. His skills were definitely passed down by his father and Klay managed to make a name for himself and break out of his father's shadow. With big shoes to fill, Klay found a way to compete against the best in college basketball. As a starter for Bennett, Klay was best known for his shooting abilities.

To play at this level, he knew that he had to improve in all facets of his game. He needed to become a better penetrator, playmaker, and defender if he wanted to survive. There was no question that Klay had great work ethic and determination. He was a little slender, so he started to hit the gym to gain some much-needed weight and strength. In his freshman year, he would average 12.5 points per game, 4.2 rebounds, 1.9 assists, 0.9 steals, and 0.6 blocks while shooting 42.1% from the field, 41.2% from range and 90.3% from the charity stripe. In his very first game, Klay would drop eight points with two 3-pointers. It was not a bad debut performance for the freshman.

Following his first game, he was up against Farleigh Dickinson scoring 9 points, grabbing 4 rebounds, dishing out 2 assists, and most impressively blocking 3 shots. Any questions pertaining to Klay's lack of defensive ability were answered by this game alone. It is not very often that a wing player can get a block in a game, but Klay was able to swat 3 of those shots in an impressive fashion.

Klay then topped his previous performance in the next game by netting 17 points with five 3-pointers, 6 rebounds, 4 assists, stealing the ball twice and blocking 1 shot. It was clear that Klay was not just a one-way player who could shoot the ball. He could definitely provide great stats all across the board when given the opportunity. Luckily for Coach Bennett and the Washington State Cougars, they had found a hidden gem in Klay.

Though they had a great start to their season, the Cougars finished off with a 17-15 record before entering the National Invitation Tournament (NIT) where they lost to St. Mary's by 11 points. Klay was named to the Pac-10 All-Freshman Team for his individual contributions, but failed to get any team recognitions worth mentioning.

Sophomore Season

Disappointed in Washington State's Men's Basketball team, Klay had to work even harder to carry his team. This proved to be difficult considering the Cougars' lack of supporting team members surrounding Klay. In his sophomore year, he boosted his numbers from the previous year. In his first two games as a sophomore, he scored a combined total of 44 points. Clearly, the Cougars needed him to produce big numbers on the offensive end in order to stand a chance. After scoring an average of 22 points per game in his first two outings, Klay managed to top his previous performances with a bang.

In his third game, Klay shot an out-of-this-world 75% from the field after posting up 20 shots. Two of these shots came from the 3-point line and he ended up finishing with a career high of 37 points in this game. He shot 75% from the field, 67% from range and 100% from the line. Not only was he amazing on the offensive end, but he also contributed in 2 steals and 1 block to go along with 3 rebounds and 3 assists. Klay showed his complete arsenal in this game and now teams were starting to take notice.

One of his most prestigious achievements while at WSU was leading the Cougars to the Great Alaska Shootout Championship. He was named Most Outstanding Player after setting a single-game record of 43 points in the championship game. This was good enough to make him third overall in WSU history for total points in a single game. He ended up finishing as the third fastest player to score 1,000 points in a WSU uniform.

Many teams began to pick up Klay from half court so he was not able to create space. Not all teams were successful in preventing Klay from doing what he does best. Klay was never static in the game, always moving on the offensive end, curling off picks and getting ready for the pass. This was Klay's best statistical career in WSU, averaging 19.6 points, 5.1 rebounds, 3.7 assists, 1.4 steals, and 0.7 blocks per game while shooting 41.2% from the field, 36.4% from range and 80% from the line. Although his percentages dropped from the 3-point line and the charity stripe, he improved in all other aspects across the board. The increased number of shots given to Klay can explain the decrease in percentages. Klay was also a candidate for the John R. Wooden Award by the end of his second year in college.

Even after a blistering 6-0 start, the Cougars again found themselves losing momentum as the season progressed. They lost the next two, but then won the next four. They then lost one and won the next two before their season started to become worse and the chance to make it to the NCAA began to dwindle away. The best record they had throughout the season was 12-3 before havoc had its way with the team. They then went 4-12 in their next 16 games, finishing off with a measly 16-15 record. Failing to make it to the NCAA tournament once again, (or any tournament, for that matter) Klay was criticized for his inability to win games.

Would Klay's legacy become tainted by his team's lack of NCAA Tournament appearances? Or would his statistical output outweigh the lack of support by his fellow teammates? Fortunately, Klay's talent helped him snag an All-Pac-10 First Team honors for his outstanding performances.

Still, Klay became frustrated by his team's inability to produce tournament-worthy performances and became even more determined to work on his own game and lead his team by example. After all, if the team noticed Klay's hard work and work ethic, then maybe that could be what would lead them into improving themselves. Klay needed more help, and it was evident. He did not let that get in his way, however. He definitely received a lot of grit from his father. Mychal was always there to help Klay in everything he did, whether it was about basketball, relationships, or school. Mychal made sure to be an important role model to Klay.

Junior and Final Season

Not only did Mychal teach his son about basketball, he was also always warning Klay to steer clear of peer pressure and bad influences. Klay took all of his dad's lessons to heart and focused most of his effort into basketball. In his first two games as a junior, Klay showcased his passing abilities and court vision, dropping 6 assists in the first game and 9 in the following. He had a little more help this year, but continued to improve on his own abilities.

He had averaged 21.6 points, 5.2 rebounds, 3.7 assists, 1.6 steals, and 0.7 blocks while shooting 43.6% from the field, 39.8% from three, and 83.8% from the line in his junior year with Washington State. Those are extremely impressive numbers for any college player to have. Klay was once again improving his previous statistics and his team ended up with a 19-12 record. This was good enough for NIT, where they made it to the semifinals after defeating Long Beach State in the first round, Oklahoma State in the second, Northwestern in the third, but then fell short to Wichita State in the semifinals. However, the biggest disappointment was Klay getting pulled over by a cop for a busted car light. The officer smelled marijuana in the vicinity and eventually found some in his car. The aforementioned event led to Klay's arrest as well as a suspension for a game against the Bruins near the end of the season. Klay's costly mistake ended up ruining the Cougars' chance to make it to the NCAA tournament. His father was extremely disappointed in him since he had always taught him to stay away from such things not only in school, but as well as in his professional life. Mychal thought he had made a big enough impact to prevent his son from making foolish choices. Klay quickly regretted the situation and learned from his mistake. The team did qualify for the NIT, which was an exciting opportunity in itself. This was WSU's best team performance with Klay in the roster. He was again named to the All-Pac-10 First Team after leading the Pac-10 in scoring. He set a new record after scoring 43 points with eight 3-pointers in the 2011 Pac-10 Tournament. Thompson finished the season with a new record of 733 points, and is WSU's third leading scorer to date. Not a bad way to end his college career. Klay then decided to enter the NBA draft where he was going to have to compete at a much higher level. This was Klay's dream coming true. His father was a two-time champion who played for the

Lakers, and it was time for his son to follow the path he had set before him.

Klay's college career set him up for a first round pick in the 2011 NBA draft. As fate had it, another Thompson would play under Jerry West. Although Mychal would have rather seen his son play for his Lakers team, the Golden State Warriors were honored to have him.

Chapter 4: Klay's NBA Career

Getting Drafted

Klay Thompson was an interesting prospect coming into the 2011 NBA Draft. Standing at nearly 6'7" and with an NBA-ready body at about 206 pounds[vi], Thompson had the size to compete with and even outmatch smaller shooting guards. He also had the size to move up to his unnatural position of small forward if the team needed him to do so. Given his good size, Klay was a very good option for any team looking for a shooting guard, especially with how skilled of a shooter he was.

Thompson was often compared to Italian shooter Marco Belinelli prior to getting drafted because of his adept shooting touch from the outside. Klay spent three years in college as arguably the best shooter in the 2011 Draft class. He was already a deadly shooter in his freshman season with Washington State University and the additional two years in college only served to further improve his shooting touch as well as the other fundamental parts of his game.

As scouting goes, the best part of Klay Thompson was always his shooting touch. Given his size at the shooting guard position and with his long arms, he could easily shoot over the defense, especially with how well he planted his feet up to spot up for three-point baskets. Klay is almost never static on the floor and always keeps moving around the court, much like NBA great shooters Reggie Miller and Ray Allen often did in their respective years. That aspect of Klay's game kept the defense adjusting and perplexed as Klay kept moving on the court and around the perimeter to find screens and open spot up looks.

The three years in college also helped Klay from a maturity standpoint, given how adept he is at making decisions. Klay Thompson rarely made bad decisions with the ball in his hands and it always seemed like he knew what he was doing. He only puts up shots he knows or at least thinks he could make and never actually developed a habit of shooting ill-advised jump shots. He's a player with limitations, but knows them well enough to not dwell on them.[vii]

When Klay is not playing off the ball, he can also create open shots for himself, even with the ball in his hands. He understands the spacing needed to get off a shot and also takes care of the ball whenever he dribbles with it. Klay is also skilled with using his pump fake to take his defenders off their feet or get them off balance for open looks at the basket or to make enough space on the floor for driving lanes. Although not an elite athlete, Klay's 6'9" wingspan makes it seem like he jumps high enough off the ground to dunk on his defenders. His wingspan also helps him defend other perimeter players, although that part of his game seems undeveloped. His long arms have a lot of potential on the defensive end, especially on contesting or blocking shots, and on picking the ball on passing lanes.[viii]

However good a shooter Klay Thompson was, he was deemed an average athlete. He could not get off the ground as high as most other NBA prospects even though he had the pedigree of an ex-NBA player and a Division I volleyball player. Along with his lack of verticality, Klay was not a very fast player and lacked the foot speed needed for teams that wanted to play the fast break as often as possible. Thus, Klay was a much better option for the half court set than on fast break situations.[ix]

Thompson was also an average player in terms of his ability to bring the basketball. His ball handling abilities did not wow anyone but they were good enough for a shooter like him. Klay was never the type of player who could break ankles with crossovers or break the defense down with his ability to penetrate to the basket with his dribble. He was someone who got open looks due to fundamentals such as using screens properly or by utilizing pump fakes. Klay's inability to break down defenses or to penetrate deep into the paint was an aspect that most scouts believed hindered him from being a solid NBA go-to guy.

Klay Thompson did not possess the ability to create plays for his other teammates and was not a very good passer, either. However, he has actually shown consistent improvement in that part of his game in his three years in college. Such an improvement was not evident enough for people to actually notice it, though. His lack in this department probably made coaches lessen his touches on the offensive end out of fear that the ball movement might get static.

Defensively, Klay was not a slacker, but needed work in that department. Even though Thompson spent three years in college, he never really developed his defense to an elite level or even to a level good enough for people to actually cite him on the defensive scouting report. Nevertheless, when Klay put his mind to that end of the court, he could actually defend properly on the ball especially when contesting shots given his long wingspan. And with 1.6 steals in his final year in

WSU, Klay has shown a good understanding of how to play the passing lanes or to anticipate the opposing players dribble.[x]

Given Klay's strengths and weaknesses, the young shooter out of Washington State was pegged to be at most a lottery pick or in the top 15 at the very least because of his advanced age (compared to other prospects) and because he was not as athletic or as successful in the college ranks as other NBA prospects. Nevertheless, Klay Thompson was too good a shooter to pass on and was someone who could make significant contributions to any team, especially to those that lacked spacing and outside shooting.

The 2011 NBA Draft class featured Kyrie Irving, Kemba Walker, Enes Kanter, Jonas Valanciunas, the Morris twins, college hotshot Jimmer Fredette, and many others. By no means was this class considered weak. Many of the players taken in this draft were up and coming freshmen that had a lot of upsides, so Klay definitely needed to stand out from the bunch.

The consensus choice for the top overall pick was the freshman out of Duke Kyrie Irving, who had a bevy of beautiful dribbling moves. The other choices were toss-ups, but the draft class had a lot of point guards to choose from. Aside from Irving, there were Brandon Knight, Kemba Walker, and Jimmer Fredette. The class also had talented big men particularly Kanter, Valanciunas, Tristan Thompson, and Bismack Biyombo. There were no other outstanding shooting guards aside from Klay Thompson, though. With that, Klay had the chance of being the highest drafted shooting guard in the draft class.

As many people expected, the Cleveland Cavaliers took Kyrie Irving as the top overall pick followed by the Timberwolves choosing power forward Derrick Williams. Three other point guards followed Irving when Knight, Walker, and Fredette were all drafted 8th, 9th, and 10th respectively. Out of the prospects that had already been chosen, only Jimmer Fredette was arguably as good a shooter as Klay was, but he was a 'tweener in that he was too unskilled to be a point guard but too short to be a shooting guard. Hence, Klay Thompson could have been the better choice as far as shooters go because of he had the size to be a shooting guard as well as the shooting stroke that goes with the position.

With the 11th pick in the draft going to the Golden State Warriors, many people pegged them to choose a defensive small forward or a big man because they already had a lot of scorers, but lacked defenders and big players. Their starting center was Andris *Biedriņš*. *Biedriņš* was in no way a scrub, but he was a role player at best. With their whole at the middle, a backcourt player was thought to be the last type of player they were going to choose considering that their backcourt positions were already filled by Stephen Curry, Monta Ellis, and Brandon Rush.

To the surprise of a lot of fans and analysts, the Golden State Warriors chose to draft Klay Thompson out of Washington State University with the 11th pick in the 2011 NBA Draft. Many thought this was not a particularly good choice considering the logjam at their backcourt positions and considering that there were defensive prospects such as Kawhi Leonard and Iman Shumpert still available. And since the Warriors sorely lacked a big man at the time, many people actually wanted them to draft big men such as one of the Morris twins or Nikola Vucevic, who were all still available.

Despite the controversial choice of picking Thompson, the Warriors front office knew what they were doing. Soon after, many analysts were beginning to see Golden State's plans. Since Golden State decided to take Klay instead of a power forward or center, many rumors of the eventual trade of Monta Ellis began to surface. Trading away Monta for a big man would have been the better choice considering he was taking away possessions from up and coming guard Stephen Curry. Furthermore, the Warriors knew that Klay was an offensive threat and that he had the tools to become a defensive-minded guard as well. The front office pegged Thompson to win the Rookie of the Year award, which gave Thompson the confidence he needed to take his talents to the next level.

Rookie Season

Since there was an obvious logjam in the backcourt of Golden State to start the season, Klay came off the bench in a reserve role. The starting shooting guard role belonged to the Warriors' leading scorer Monta Ellis. Ellis was a very good scorer and consistently scored more than 20 points per game. However, he was a player who needed the ball in his hands all the time and was undersized. Hence, Klay was eyed to be a player who could take away that spot from Ellis in the future.

In Klay's rookie year, the Warriors were far from being a contender in the West. Golden State was a team that was undergoing ownership transitions and had a lot of young players on the roster. The team was talented on the offensive end but performed poorly in the defensive end of the court. With that fact in mind, nobody expected them to achieve very much in the coming seasons, even with newly drafted shooter Klay Thompson in the lineup.

During his first NBA game, Thompson managed to score 7 points with 3 rebounds and 1 assist in just 19 minutes of action. Statistically, he didn't have the most efficient night shooting, scoring 2 for 8 from the field, turning the ball over twice and committing 3 personal fouls. The stage was set for Thompson to show what he could really do, but transitioning into the "big boy's league" was proving to be more difficult than he imagined.

His next four performances were not the greatest, either. With a short amount of minutes played, it was difficult for Klay to develop any rhythm or chemistry with the unit. He failed to top his first game performance of 7 points and continued his trend of poor shooting, turnover collection, and committing unnecessary fouls. He was learning as he played, but with sheer determination and great work ethic, Klay finally pulled in a couple of games scoring in the double digits. Mind you, he did this while shooting a combined 10 of 18, which was a good sign for both the Warriors and himself.

Throughout his rookie year, his inconsistent performances continued. He was in a reserve role for the majority of the season, never playing more than 23 minutes in a game as a backup for Ellis or as a small forward, a position he was not very accustomed to playing. As fate had it, the Warriors had the opportunity to trade Ellis to the Bucks in exchange for Aussie center Andrew Bogut. Even with Bogut's extensive injury history, the Warriors decided to pull the trigger and trade big in the hopes of adding a key defensive piece to their frontcourt and in order to free up the backcourt for Stephen Curry and Klay Thompson. The team also acquired Jarrett Jack midseason to play as a backup point guard and as a mentor for younger Warrior guards.

Following this trade, Klay was inserted into the starting lineup and scored a season high 26 points against the Celtics. One week later he topped his previous season high with 27 points and 31 points two games after that. This was a dawning of a new era as Klay scored double digits the rest of the way (with the exception of one game). He was definitely gaining a lot of confidence, and Coach Jackson was encouraging it. Klay formed a dynamic duo with Stephen Curry and eventually they were dubbed as the "Splash Brothers." Although the Warriors failed to make it to the playoffs with a poor win-loss record of 23-43 in a lockout-shortened season, Klay was voted to the NBA All-Rookie First Team. With much grit, determination, and a sudden change in the starting lineup, Klay was finally able to show the world what he could do when given the opportunity. Klay was playing at a high level and averaged 12.5 points, 2.4 rebounds, 2.0 assists, 0.7

steals and 0.3 blocks while shooting 44% from the field, 41% from range, and 87% from the charity stripe.

Full-Time Starter

After having one year of experience under his belt, Klay was looking to develop his numbers. Determined to be considered as more than just a one-trick pony, Klay worked on his ball handling and defense. His idols growing up were Alan Houston, Penny Hardaway, and Kobe Bryant, all of whom were two-way players. In order for Klay to become more like his childhood idols, he knew he had his work cut out for him.

The 2012 offseason was also the start of a new generation of players for the Warriors. Following their dismal 2011-12 season, they managed to draft small forward Harrison Barnes as the 7th overall pick. The Warriors lacked depth at that position which pegged Barnes to be the starter right away. They then drafted big man Festus Ezeli with the final pick in the first round of the draft. Festus would prove to be a good addition given the injury history of Andrew Bogut. In the second round of the 2012 Draft, the Warriors chose to bring in unheralded forward Draymond Green who would prove to be a very big steal for the Golden State franchise. They also added frontcourt depth by signing veteran forward Carl Landry in free agency. Unfortunately, their big gamble Andrew Bogut was still unavailable for most of the upcoming season as he was still recovering from his injuries. The rookie Festus Ezeli had to start instead. Thankfully, the young Warriors were up to the challenge even without their starting center and even with two rookies in the starting lineup.

In his second year, Klay was looking to continue with his previous success. He became the starting shooting guard for the Golden State Warriors along with much-improved point guard Stephen Curry. He was scoring in the double digits in his first seven games, but was shooting no more than 42% in any of those games.

Klay had stretches of scoring in double digits as well as less spectacular games to follow suit. He was trying to be as consistent as he could be throughout the whole season, and improved in virtually all facets of his game statistically. Still, Klay was a little bit of an inconsistent player. But when he got hot, it was almost impossible for him to miss shots. However, when he was cold, he struggled.

It was in his sophomore year that which Coach Jackson claimed that Klay and Stephen were to become one of the best shooting duos in NBA history. These are definitely strong words coming from a coach who used to play in the NBA himself. Jackson competed during a time that some might consider as the best era in NBA history. Having to go up against the likes of Michael Jordan, Gary Payton, Isaiah Thomas, and Clyde Drexler was not the easiest of tasks to complete. Mark Jackson also competed against the Run TMC era of the Warriors in the early 90's. To have Jackson say that his two backcourt players could be one of the greatest shooting duos in NBA history says volumes about Klay and Stephen. Klay and Stephen were also two members (together with David Lee) of one of the highest scoring trio in the NBA at that time. With the trio leading the team, the Warriors were an increasing offensive threat and were greatly improving from seasons past.

Jackson was not so farfetched in his statement as Curry and Thompson combined for a total of 483 3-point shots, setting a new NBA record. The duo splashed their way into the record books and led their team to their first ever playoff appearance together. They easily broke the record formerly held by the Magic duo of Dennis Scott and Nick Anderson back in the 90's. Stephen Curry led the highlights for the duo by hitting a total of 272 three-point baskets the entire season. That number broke a record previously held by Ray Allen. Curry would later break his own record. Klay Thompson ended the regular season averaging 16.6 points, 3.7 rebounds, and 1 steal per game while shooting 42 percent from the floor, 40 percent on three-pointers, and 84 percent from free throws. He also hit a ton of three-point baskets with a total of 211. With the leadership of the young shooting tandem, the Golden State Warriors were able to end the season with a 47-35 win-loss record, which was a 24-win improvement from the previous season. They were good enough to make the 6th seed of the playoffs for the ultra-competitive Western Conference.

During the first round of the playoffs, the Warriors found themselves in a war against the high performance Denver Nuggets. Golden State was the underdog in this matchup, but they didn't let that take away from their game plan. With an exciting first game underway, the Nuggets and Warriors traded blows. Both teams were used to up-tempo games with high scores, but this one was slightly different. Klay led his team with 22 points. Lee got hurt during this game which forced rookie Draymond Green to step into his place.

The Michigan State alumni was trying his best to fill the void left by Lee. This game ended up coming down to the wire as Curry hit a corner 3-point shot to tie it up at 95 with 14.5 seconds left on the clock. The next play on the other side, Miller found himself being guarded by Draymond Green. Although Andre Miller had lost a step, the savvy veteran point guard made a couple of moves to get himself to the rim and hit a layup with 1.2 seconds left on the clock. This ended up being the winning shot with Denver taking game number one. Nonetheless, Klay became the youngest player in Warriors history to score 22 points in a playoff game. Game 2 was a higher tempo game than the previous nail-biter. Unlike the first game, both teams came out of the block shooting the ball well. Curry did not have a slow start like he had in the previous game, and ended up leading the team with 30 points. To combat the Nuggets' style of small ball, the Warriors inserted Jarrett Jack into the starting lineup. With a lineup of Curry, Thompson, Jack, Barnes, and Bogut, the

Warriors were able to match the speed of the Nuggets. Four out of the five starters on the Warriors finished with 20 or more points, with Klay himself making 21 points. The Warriors played small ball the whole way through and beat the Nuggets at their own game. The Nuggets could not answer back to the Warriors' starting unit and Golden State beat the Nuggets 131-117.

The third game at home in the Warriors' floor turned out to be Klay's worst game of the season. He only scored 6 points in 35 minutes. The Warriors used the same starting five as the previous game, but with Thompson lacking in production, they needed someone else to step up. Carl Landry rose up from the shadows and scored 19 much-needed points to keep up with the Nuggets. Harrison Barnes' free throws gave the Warriors a two-point lead with only three seconds left on the clock. With no timeouts left to advance the ball, the Nuggets had to go full-court to tie it up or win the game. Iguodala rose up for a half-court heave, but fell short of the victory. The Warriors also took game 4 in a dominating fashion and jumped up to a 3-1 lead over the Nuggets by winning three straight games. Despite the Warriors' attempts in game five, Denver finally won a game after winning the opener to make the series 3-2.

Game 6 was played at home for the Warriors, where they had a chance to win the series with their sea of yellow-clad fans cheering them on. This game was much different than the others with a much lower than average score. Bogut proved to be the X-factor by scoring 14 points, grabbing 21 rebounds and swatting away 4 shots. Klay did not perform very well in this matchup, shooting 3-13 and finishing with only 7 points. The Warriors led the Nuggets 80-62 with nine minutes left, but the Nuggets then tightened up their defense and pulled a comeback, getting them as close as 4 points with four minutes left. However, the Warriors proved to be too much for the Nuggets, as they lost in an upset by the 6th seed in the first round of the playoffs. The Warriors were moving on to face the Spurs in the next round.

The Spurs were a formidable opponent who easily dismantled Mychal Thompson's LA Lakers in a series sweep. San Antonio had plenty of time to rest and focus on their next matchup against the Warriors. The first game of the series proved to be nothing less than spectacular. Two Western Conference heavy-hitters went toe-to-toe in an epic clash of David and Goliath, but would the story rewrite history? The Warriors had their way with the Spurs through the first three quarters and led by 16 points with only 4:20 left on the clock. The Spurs pulled together and went on an 18-2 run with Klay Thompson fouling out of the game. This proved to be quite costly for the Warriors and the Spurs would tie it up and make the game go into overtime.

Without Thompson, Curry had to shoulder more of the offensive output, finishing with 44 points and 11 assists in over 50 minutes of action. The suspense carried over to a second overtime where the Warriors were up 2 points with just a few seconds left on the clock. However, Manu Ginobili found himself wide open for a 3-pointer and sank it with just 1.2 seconds left. Goliath ended up winning this game in an impressive fashion and this led to a very exciting series matchup with Klay Thompson and the Warriors. After a disappointing loss, Klay looked to improve on his first performance against the Spurs. He followed up his mediocre game with a career and playoff high of 34 points and 14 rebounds, as well as shooting 8-9 from deep. This showed Klay's determination and will to constantly progress. This was his first career playoff double-double and it greatly helped the Warriors to take game 2 away from the Spurs. Both the Warriors and Spurs took one game apiece before the Spurs had their way in the following two games. San Antonio was just too experienced for the team to overcome and the Warriors' shooting duo could not erupt at the same time to save the day for their team.

The Spurs eventually swept the Memphis Grizzlies in the Western Conference finals. They ended up losing to Miami in game seven after a miraculous game-tying shot by Ray Allen in the dwindling minutes of game 6. This was the first playoff appearance for the Warriors in a very long time, and they were able to exceed expectations. Klay Thompson did not perform as well in the playoffs as he did in the regular season. He averaged 15.2 points, 4.6 rebounds, and 1 steal per game while shooting 42 percent from three-point territory. Not bad for his first playoff appearance.

The Rise of Klay Thompson

The Warriors had gained much needed experience in the playoffs and were looking to rebuild going into the next year. That was the first playoff run that the Splash Brothers duo of Steph Curry and Klay Thompson played together. Despite being their first, they were able to impress a lot of people. They beat a third-seeded Denver Nuggets who had home court advantage. They then put up a tough but futile fight against the veteran and championship-tested San Antonio Spurs team. It was an experience that helped the team get to the next level.

The Warriors looked to improve their team exponentially. They nabbed the veteran do-it-all small forward Andre Iguodala from the free agency market for a four-year contract worth $48 million. They then traded away the large contracts of Richard Jefferson and Biedriņš to make more room for free agency signings. Although they would lose their big-time sixth man point guard Jarrett Jack and back-up power forward Carl Landry, they were able to make up for it since Iguodala was also a good playmaker and because they were able to sign big man Marreese Speights to a relatively cheap contract. Iguodala immediately became the starting small forward and Speights played big minutes behind David Lee and Andrew Bogut. Klay, as per usual, bested his statistical performance from the previous year. His drive and work ethic is above average in the NBA, and it shows by the way he constantly improves every single year. On opening night, Klay dropped a career high 38 points shooting 5-7 from deep. Thompson and Curry continued with their Splash Brothers dominance from range. They tortured their opponents with a 3-point spectacle. Coach Jackson was not so far off when he claimed that they are the best shooting duo in NBA history and they've proven that fact by constantly being the top three-point shooting duo in the league. It was during this season where they beat their NBA record of combined 3's in a regular season.

Klay started to develop into one of the best shooting guards in the NBA. He found himself in some good company with Bryant, Harden, and Wade just ahead of him. Although only 2 of the 3 players in front of him were two-way players, Harden was just magnificent offensively, which placed him above Klay. Klay Thompson and James Harden had met back in high school. Back then, Harden was miles ahead of Klay.

However, at this point in Klay's career, he was closing the gap and was the better defensive player.

Despite the rise of Klay Thompson into a big time shooting guard and of Stephen Curry into an All-Star player, the Warriors had a lot of lapses, especially because of injuries.

The Warriors made a move to trade for Steve Blake as a backup for Curry. And when the injuries that the team faced were all but gone, the Warriors were able to win 10 straight games, which was the highest streak for a struggling Golden State franchise since their last championship in 1975. With the improvements to the team and with the rise of their young core players, the Golden State franchise won 51 games to just 31 losses. It was the first time that the Warriors won more than 50 games since 1992. The Warriors made it to the playoffs with, again, the sixth seed. It was the first time since 1992 that the Warriors made consecutive trips to the playoffs. They were going up against the third-seeded Los Angeles Clippers. At the end of the season, Thompson had improved his numbers. He normed 18.4 points, 3.1 rebounds, and 2.2 dimes per game while shooting almost 42% from three-point territory.

If you went back five seasons, you would laugh at the idea of the Warriors and the Clippers facing each other in the playoffs. After all, neither of those teams had any history of regular season success, much less in the playoffs. However, in the 2014 playoffs, both the Warriors and the Clippers were much improved and were no longer the laughing stock franchises they were in previous years. The Warriors had a good young core of shooters while the Clippers two All-Star point guard Chris Paul and power forward Blake Griffin, both of whom were among the best at their respective positions.

Klay Thompson was instrumental when the Warriors stole game one and home court advantage away from the Clippers. The Warriors were heading into the opening game wounded without their best rebounder and interior defender, Andrew Bogut. Moreover, the Clippers held the lead entering the fourth quarter and were undefeated in that regard. However, Golden State mounted a furious rally in the second half to win the game 109 to 105. Klay Thompson top scored for his team with 22 points including 4 out 7 from three-point range. Meanwhile, Chris Paul scored 28 for the Clippers.

Unfortunately for the Warriors, the Clippers were in no mood to lose two straight games on their home floor. They recorded a franchise-high for most points in a playoff game and the largest winning margin they'd had in the post season. The Clippers won the game 138 to 98 and blew the Warriors out with a 40-point margin. Seven Clippers were in double digits led by the 35 points of Blake Griffin. Meanwhile, Klay Thompson struggled all night long and only had 7 points in 20 minutes of action. Stephen Curry scored 24 to lead his Warriors.

Game three was on the Warriors home floor with both teams refusing to give in to each other. The Warriors were once again down by a considerable amount entering the fourth quarter, but mounted another rally. It was for naught though, because the Clippers were able to hold on to a two-point victory and regained home court advantage. Once again, Blake Griffin pounded the Warriors' inside defense with 32 points. DeAndre Jordan had 22 rebounds and it was evident that Golden State was missing the services of Andrew Bogut. Klay Thompson bounced back from a dismal performance with 26 points. Curry had 16 points and 15 assists.

The Warriors quickly bounced back in their second home game. They gave everything they had to the Clippers from the opening tip and ran Los Angeles out of the arena with 27 fast break points. Steph Curry exploded for 33 points on 7 out of 14 three-point shots. Klay had a respectable 15-point performance and hit 3 three-pointers. He only played 29 minutes in the blowout 118-97 victory.

Game five back in Los Angeles was a different story. The Warriors were once again overwhelmed by the inside presence of the Clippers as Golden State opted to go smaller with Lee at the center and Draymond Green at the power forward spot. This strategy allowed them to play faster, but really depleted their inside defense and rebounding. Jordan lorded over the boards with 18 and also had 25 points. Klay Thompson led the Warriors, who lost 103-113, with 21 points while also hitting three rainbow shots. Golden State suddenly found themselves in a 3-2 hole and were one loss away from elimination.

In another tight one in Oakland, the Warriors were able to stave off elimination by winning 100-99 in the tightest of margins. Stephen Curry broke out from a shooting slump and scored 24 points. Meanwhile, Klay struggled with only 9 points on 3 of 11 shooting. The

Warriors were now in a do-or-die game seven in the hostile territory of Los Angeles.

Game seven became a shootout and neither team would allow the other to outshoot them the entire game. It was a game of runs that featured a strong first half from the Warriors followed by an equally mighty second half rally by the Clippers. In the end, the Warriors lost to the Clippers 121 to 126. The Clipper bench led by the 22 points of Jamal Crawford was the difference-maker in the game. Four Clippers scored more than 20. Meanwhile, Curry was a one-man show with 33 points. Klay struggled in the elimination game with only 15 points on 4 out of 11 shooting from the field.

Unlike the previous season, the Warriors failed to do any serious damage in the playoffs and were unable to make a deep run despite a much-improved team. Because of the elimination and because of how Mark Jackson could not see eye-to-eye with team ownership, the Golden State Warriors were headed to an offseason full of questions and new faces.

Championship Season

Following their first round playoff exit the previous season, Klay and Curry joined Team USA. His experience on Team USA really helped to shape Klay's career. He found himself competing for a spot on the roster against the likes of Chandler Parsons, DeMar DeRozan, James Harden, and Paul George. After George suffered a gruesome injury, Klay's chances of making the team greatly increased. He ended up making the team based on his dominating performance in the tournament, capturing the gold medal for the red, white, and blue (Team USA). The FIBA three-point line was too short for a knockdown shooter like Klay Thompson. He ended up averaging 12.7 points on 42% shooting from the field as one of the top scorers for Team USA.

It was during this time when rumors of a Kevin Love for Klay Thompson package began to surface. Although the Warriors were hesitant to trade an up-and-coming player in Thompson, to receive someone like Kevin Love in return was definitely an upgrade. Love was also a shooter like Thompson, but played a different position. He would have played the role of floor-spacer for the Warriors. Luckily, the trade did not go through and it was Cleveland who ended up acquiring Love. This did not bother Klay much since he was still in his Warriors uniform to start the year. The Golden State Warriors also went through a transition in the offseason. There were differences in how the Golden State front office saw the team's future and how it worked with the philosophies of head coach Mark Jackson. With that, Jackson was fired. This was, at the start, a huge blow to the Warriors because Mark Jackson was responsible for bringing the team back into playoff contention after making the playoffs only once in the last 17 years since Jackson

71

had taken over the team. He was also responsible for a large part in the development of Klay and Curry by instilling in them the confidence and the offensive reigns of a jump-shooting team.

It was former TNT analyst Steve Kerr who took over the Warriors' coaching reigns. Kerr was a multiple-time NBA champion in his playing years and had the pleasure to play with Michael Jordan in Chicago and for legendary coaches such as Phil Jackson and Gregg Popovich. Despite Kerr's apparent experience as an analyst and as a former player, he never had the pleasure of being a coach on any professional basketball team. He was immediately given the head coaching duties of a young and inexperienced team. This led to many people speculating that the Warriors would once again fall into limbo in the transition period with Steve Kerr.

Klay was in his last year of his rookie contract and was looking to strike a deal for a contract extension. On October 31st, 2014, Klay signed a contract extension worth $70 million for four years. It was heavily debated as an overpayment and Klay must have heard the whispers throughout the NBA. After all, whispers travel fast in the NBA and are difficult to ignore. He followed up his contract extension with a career high of 41 points the next day, against his father's favorite team: the LA Lakers. When you watch this game, you can see Klay become more mature. Kobe Bryant couldn't help but take notice as Klay had an epic performance. It was as if it was a "passing of the torch" moment. Not to say that Klay is considered the best SG in the NBA, but he is definitely in the top 5. Having Kobe praise Thompson for his play solidified Klay's place in the NBA. It's not very often that Kobe says anything nice about any player who is not on the Lakers. It was Klay's idol growing up who was showing much respect for the way Klay played the game. It couldn't have been a happier moment in Klay's life.

Furthermore, the Golden State Warriors did not struggle under Steve Kerr. In fact, they flourished. Kerr brought a different philosophy to the team and instilled in them the tenets of great teamwork and ball movement. The Warriors immediately looked reminiscent of the Spurs, especially when they moved the ball around the court. They were passing the ball around so fast and so much that it was easy for Klay Thompson and Stephen Curry to get open looks at the basket.

A lot of players also made sacrifices for the sake of the team. Steve Kerr talked to Andre Iguodala prior to the season and asked him to play the role of the sixth man off the bench. The starting small forward role was given to Harrison Barnes. Iggy would not reject the role change and, in fact, embraced it despite starting almost all of the games in his entire NBA career. He would not start a single regular season game as a Warrior after Kerr took over. However, Andre Iguodala's presence in the second half along with key offseason pickups Shaun Livingston and Leandro Barbosa was what made the Warriors a good team the entire 48 minutes.

Next, when David Lee went down early in the season with an injury, Kerr opted to insert Draymond Green to the starting squad. This would prove to be one of the best moves that the Warriors made the entire season. While Lee was a terrific offensive threat and a very good rebounder, he was limited as a defender and playmaker. Draymond, on the other hand, evolved into an excellent all-around defender both out on the perimeter and on the post. Offensively, Green could handle the ball and make plays for his teammates with his passing abilities. He also lost a lot of weight over the offseason and became much faster for opposing power forwards. Moreover, he had more shooting range than David Lee. Even as Lee fully recovered from his injury, the starting spot was already given to Green for the rest of the season.

The Warriors quickly started the season with the best record in the NBA and were playing much better than the usual powerhouses such as the San Antonio Spurs and the OKC Thunder. They were so good the entire regular season that the only team that had a record consistently close to the Warriors was the Hawks team over in Atlanta. Stephen Curry immediately raced ahead to become the top MVP contender and Steven Kerr became a contender for Coach of the Year.

For Klay Thompson, the improved ball movement and floor spacing helped him get off his shots with ease and with less defensive pressure. He was the solid second option for the team despite a lot of ball movement being involved. Klay was consistent in shooting the ball, something he was often criticized for in the past, because a lot of pressure was alleviated from him.

On January 23, 2015, Klay Thompson made NBA history. He scored 37 points in a single quarter against the Sacramento Kings. He almost seemed unconscious as soon as the third quarter started. It became an out of body experience as Klay just could not miss from the field despite jacking up far away shots or shooting in front of the outstretched arms of his defender. He went 13 out of 13 from the field in that quarter and also hit 9 three-pointers, which was the record for most three-point shots in a single quarter. Not too many players even get to score 37 in four quarters. Klay did it in just one. When Klay is hot, it is almost impossible for him to miss. He ended that night with 52 points, and obviously could have scored a lot more if they did not blow the Kings out so early.

Klay Thompson's explosion in that game along with his steady shooting and scoring throughout the year earned him the attention of the NBA. The coaches voted him in as a reserve player in the Western Conference All-Star team. It was Klay's first All-Star appearance in his NBA career. His backcourt buddy Stephen Curry was an All-Star starter that season. Klay recorded 7 points in almost 20 minutes of play as an All-Star.

The leadership of the two Warrior All-Stars along with the improved play of Draymond Green and the sacrifices of Iguodala catapulted the Golden State Warriors to an amazing 67-15 win-loss record for the entire regular season. The Splash Brothers reset their league record for most three-pointers by a duo with 484. Curry broke his own record with 261 made threes while Thompson had the rest of the 223 three-pointers. At the end of the season, Klay had career highs in almost every statistical category despite playing only 32 minutes, the lowest amount of minutes since his rookie year. He averaged 21.7 points, 3.2 rebounds, 2.9 assists, and 1.1 steals per game while shooting 46 percent from the floor and 43.7 percent from three-point territory. Meanwhile, Curry was voted as the NBA's Most Valuable Player, the only other Warriors player out of two to win the award. The Warriors team had the best record in the league and had home court advantage the entire playoffs.

In the first round, the Warriors went up with the young and inexperienced New Orleans Pelicans, who only managed to get the playoff spot in the last minute of the regular season. Despite their opponent's inexperience, the Warriors did not put them away easily in the opening game. The Warriors raced to a quick first half lead, but the Pelicans cut it down in the fourth quarter. The Warriors used their superior talent and experience to hold on to the 106-99 win. Curry top scored with 34 while Klay had 21 on 3 out of 6 shooting from three.

Game two was more of the same. The Pelicans were gritty but the Warriors were just too good to let a game slip up. Golden State won the game and held off every rally that the Pelicans mustered. Klay led the Warriors with 26 points while the young and ultra-talented big man Anthony Davis led the Pelicans with 26. With the win, the Warriors quickly gained a commanding 2-0 win over the Pelicans and were poised to quickly finish the second round.

Game three in New Orleans was an instant NBA classic. The Warriors found themselves in a 20-point hole dug open by the Pelicans' dynamic play. However, the Warriors suddenly turned it around and owned the fourth quarter, founded upon the spectacular play of their Splash Brothers. In the dying seconds, the Pelicans were up by three and the Warriors had possession. Stephen Curry found an opening at the left corner to shoot a three-pointer, but missed. Mo Speights got the offensive rebound and quickly brought it back to Curry in the same corner. Stephen put up the shot as quickly as he could and drained it to send the game into overtime. The Warriors put the Pelicans down in the extra period and suddenly had a commanding and insurmountable 3-0 series lead. Curry had 40 points including the game saving three-pointer while Klay Thompson had 28 on 6 out 12 three-point shooting. The Pelicans were so disheartened that they could no longer put up a fight in game four. Stephen Curry ended the series sweep with 39 points and solidified his name as the MVP of the league.

In the second round, the Warriors faced the grittiest and one of the most physical teams in the NBA. The Memphis Grizzlies prided themselves on the way they pressured the ball handler to force turnovers and on the way they loved grinding the ball down at the low post with their physical big men. The Warriors were a top offensive team relying on jump shots and outside shooting. Meanwhile, the Grizzlies were a tough defensive squad relying on inside scoring. It was indeed a meeting of the opposites. As the saying goes, offense wins games, but defense wins championships. The Warriors were the best offensive team but were up against arguably the toughest NBA defense. Another saying goes that better offense always trumps over great defense, though. Did the Warriors have an offense good enough to beat the Memphis defense?

Klay Thompson and the Warriors were not at all intimidated by the defensive prowess of the Grizzlies. They started off game one with a strong first half led by the two most prominent shooters on the planet. They further compounded their lead with a dominant third quarter and the Warriors took care of business on their home floor in game one. Klay Thompson and Stephen Curry led the way with 18 and 22 points respectively while combining for 6 out of 13 from downtown to win the game 101 to 86 against the Grizzlies without their starting point guard, Mike Conley.

Mike Conley returned in game two and provided the inspirational spark against the Warriors. Thompson and Curry could not get a pass or shoot above the tough perimeter defense of Memphis now that Conley, their top defensive point guard, was back in the flow of the lineup. Curry only had 19 on 7 out of 19 shooting while Klay scored 13 points on a poor 6 out of 15. The two only combined for 3 out of 17 from three-point territory. Meanwhile, Mike Conley and Courtney Lee outscored their matchups by putting up 22 and 15 respectively. The Warriors just could not score against the Grizzlies and ended up falling 90 to 97. With the loss, home court advantage now belonged to Memphis. The series was off to Memphis where the Warriors were in danger of falling 1-3 in the series with the two home games for the Grizzlies. As good as the Warriors were in the regular season, they had not been tested well in the playoffs, especially against the top-tier defensive squads such as Memphis. The Grizzlies were able to protect the first game on their home floor by going back to their grit-and-grind style of defense and inside scoring. Although Curry and Klay were able to score more than 20 points each, the inside defense of the Warriors could not hold off the physical big men duo of the Grizzlies. Gasol and Randolph combined for 43 each to match the 43 of the Splash Brothers. The other Memphis starters stepped up to win the game by 10 points. The Warriors were suddenly in a hole and in danger of letting the series slip away. Rallying on the inspirational motivation given by Coach Steve Kerr, the Golden State Warriors suddenly found the intensity they needed to fight back against the Memphis Grizzlies. The Warriors immediately gave the fight to the home team in the first half with Curry scoring 22 in the first 24 minutes. The Warriors were able to hold on to the first half lead they had built and got back their home court advantage with a 17-point victory in Memphis. Curry had 33 points while Thompson scored 15 including 3 out of 6 from downtown.

With the series tied at two wins apiece heading back into Oakland, the Warriors found renewed vigor and energy to keep their championship hopes alive. The Oracle Arena was alive and kicking to cheer on their squad as the Warriors won all four quarters against Memphis to race on to a 3-2 lead over the series. In the 98-78 victory, Klay Thompson was the top man with

21 points while shooting 3 out 4 from his favorite spot. His buddy Curry had 18 points all on three-pointers. Just two games before, the Warriors were being criticized for not being able to win against a tough defensive team like the Grizzlies. They were in danger of letting the series and their historic season go. In game six though, they were just one win away from heading to the Western Conference Finals. Not wanting a seventh and deciding game against a veteran team such as the Grizzlies, the Warriors put on their running shoes and raced to a fast first half performance. At the end of the third quarter, just when Memphis was beginning to rally, Curry suddenly hit an MVP buzzer-beater to quell the Memphis run. With their eyes set on making the playoff semi-finals, Klay and Curry shot their way to a 108-95 victory to end the series and the hopes of the Grizzlies. Curry had 32 points to lead the game including 8 three-point shots. Klay Thompson was very efficient with 20 points on 7 out 13 shooting and 3 out of 5 from downtown. For the first time in a

very long time, the Golden State Warriors found themselves competing for a Finals spot.

The road to the finals did not get any easier. The Warriors were matched up against an equally talented Houston Rockets team that had just completed a monumental comeback against the Clippers to reach the West Finals. The Rockets were led by dominant big man Dwight Howard and scoring specialist James Harden, who finished second to Curry in MVP voting and was once Klay Thompson's tormentor in high school. Fate indeed has a way of intertwining people's paths together.

The Warriors refused to let James Harden get his revenge for having finished second in the MVP voting. Harden believed he was the MVP and the best shooting guard in the NBA. However, the Warriors had the official MVP and the other player contending for the spot of best shooting guard. To start the game, the Rockets were intent on stealing one at Oakland but the Warriors rallied in the second quarter from a 16-

point deficit due to Shaun Livingston's scoring. He had 18 the entire game. Klay Thompson found himself guarding the MVP runner-up the entire game and did not give him room to drive or shoot. Nevertheless, Harden was a prominent scorer and still found ways to get points up. He had 28 for the game. Meanwhile, Curry exploded for 34 to cement his name as the rightful MVP. Focusing on defense, Thompson had 15 points for the Warriors who won 110-106.

Despite the "in your face" defense played by Klay on James Harden, the Bearded shooting guard still scored 38 points in game two. The Rockets were down by as much as 17 points in the first half on the strength of James' immaculate scoring abilities. However, it was a last play fumble on the part of Harden that sealed the game for Golden State. Up by one point in the final seconds and with Houston with the possession, the Splash Brothers suddenly doubled up on Harden just as he got the ball past mid-court. The double team pressured the bearded one and forced a turnover on his part to seal the one-point victory for the Warriors. Klay and Golden State protected the Oracle Arena and were up 2-0 heading into Houston.

People expected a lot of fight from the Rockets on their home court and especially with how Harden made mincemeat out of Klay Thompson's defense in the first two games. Klay finally got the best of him in the first game on the Rocket's home floor. Harden was limited to just 17 points on a dismal 3 out 16 shooting. Meanwhile, Klay had 17 of his own on a better shooting clip than Harden. The story of the game was the 40-point output of MVP Stephen Curry who shot 7 out of 9 from three-point territory to secure a blowout 115-80 victory on the part of Golden State.

Up 3-0 in the series, the Golden State Warriors were virtual winners of the series and had the NBA Finals berth all but taken care of. Klay and his backcourt partner already smelled their first Finals appearance. Harden had other plans though, and decided to extend the series to at least one more game. The Beard exploded for 45 points and was shooting tough step-back shots in the face of Klay Thompson's defense. He had 7 three-pointers for the whole game. Klay and Curry both scored 20+ points and hit 6 three-pointers each, but they could not stop the Rockets from scoring at will to lose the game 115 to 128.

Back in Oakland, the Warriors started the first quarter slowly and it looked as if the Rockets were once again poised to extend the series to one more game. The Warriors were more poised than their counterparts in red, though. Golden State rallied beginning in the second quarter and practically owned the rest of the game to win it by 14. After his 45-point outburst, James Harden was suddenly feeling the defensive pressure of Klay and Iguodala out on the perimeter. He was limited to merely 14 points on 2 out 11 shooting. The worst part of it was his 12 turnovers forced by the pesky hands of both Klay and Iggy. It was an all-around effort on the part of the Warriors. Curry, Barnes, and Thompson all scored 20+ points with 26,

24, and 20 points respectively. The Splash Brothers and the Warriors finally ended the franchise's 40-year NBA Finals drought. The last time they had been in the Finals was in 1975. They won that year to secure the team's then-lone championship banner.

The Golden State Warriors were in a good situation to win a second franchise championship banner, especially with how well they'd played in the regular season and in the playoffs. Things could not have been more difficult though as Klay and the Warriors were set to square off for the golden trophy against the Cleveland Cavaliers. It was the first year of LeBron James in a Cavaliers uniform since coming back to the team via the 2014 free agency. It was also LeBron's fifth straight NBA Finals appearance, giving him more championship experience than the whole Warriors roster. Moreover, he had an All-Star point guard Kyrie Irving, who handles the ball just as well as Stephen Curry and could score just as explosively as any other player in the league.

The Warriors threw a lot of defenders to try to bother LeBron James at the start of the Finals series. LeBron saw Harrison Barnes, Andre Iguodala, and Draymond Green all trying to stop him from imposing his will. James was able to score 44 points on 18 out of 38 shooting in game one. LeBron's terrific play got the Cavs a double-digit lead at the start of the game, but the Warriors gradually chipped into that lead. With the game tied in the final seconds, Curry had the ball and slipped past Irving. Just when Curry was about to go up for an uncontested layup, Irving got up on his feet and blocked the shot. The game went into overtime and the Warriors buckled up on defense to limit Cleveland and LeBron to merely 2 points in the extra period to win the game 108 to 100. Stephen Curry led the Warriors with 26 points followed by the 21 of Klay, who played defense on Irving for most of the game. The Warriors got a bit of luck coming into game two. Kyrie Irving suffered a serious injury in game one and had to miss the rest of the Finals series. The Dubs suddenly found themselves one less dynamic player to guard. It did not seem as if the Cavs missed their All-Star point man, though. They rallied to the 39-point triple-double output of the planet's best player. Although LeBron shot only 11 out of 35, he did everything else right. He got his center Timofey Mozgov involved in the scoring parade and he also lorded over the rebounds. Moreover, backup point guard Matthew Dellavedova played the best possible defense anyone can play on Stephen Curry. The MVP was limited to just 19 points on 5-23 from the field and 2-15 from three-point territory. It was Klay who picked up the scoring cudgels after not having to defend a solid perimeter player. He had 34 points but it was for naught as the Warriors fell game two at home 93 to 95.

With the series tied at one game apiece, it was now the Warriors' turn to try to steal a home game away from Cleveland. Once again, LeBron James could not be stopped from scoring at will. He scored 40 points the second time around in the series but shot only 14 out of 34. Despite the bad shooting numbers, he did have 12 rebounds and 8 assists to win the game 96-91. The Cavs had the game under control until a fourth quarter rally mounted by the Warriors cut the lead down to more manageable numbers. The Warriors did not have enough in their tank to take the lead and win the game, though. Curry broke out from a shooting slump and had 27 points and 7 three-point shots made. Klay had 14 on 6 out 16 shooting for the Warriors who were suddenly down 1-2 in the series and were only two losses away from losing the Finals.

Knowing that his game plan in the past three games did not work as well as he thought, Steve Kerr made lineup changes coming into game four. He suddenly inserted Andre Iguodala into the starting squad to replace Andrew Bogut. Draymond Green was set to play center, but the Warriors were too small against the big Cavs frontcourt. However, small-ball was what the Warriors needed to get back into the series. With the floor stretched open and with the Warriors playing faster, Golden State ran Cleveland out of their own building. Though Mozgov dominated inside the paint with 28 points, Iguodala's defense on LeBron limited the King to only 20 points on 7 out of 22 from the field. It was Iggy's first time to start the whole season and it immediately paid dividends to win the game by 21 points. He scored 22 to tie the same output of Curry. Meanwhile, Klay Thompson had only 9 points but only shot 9 times to focus on playing defense and as the floor stretcher.

Game five in Oakland started tight with the Dubs merely leading by a single point heading into halftime. Yet they suddenly found the offensive accelerator to pull away from the Cavs come the second half. The Warriors just survived the 40 points, 14 rebounds, and 11 assists of the triple-double machine LeBron James. Although the King could not be stopped, his teammates were practically invisible. Meanwhile, Curry's 37 points got a lot of help from all of the other

Warriors. Klay had 12, Green scored 16, and Barbosa off the bench had 13. Golden State suddenly gained hold of the series lead 3-2 and were only one win away from ending the Franchise's 40-year title drought.

In the sixth game, LeBron James once again did everything for his team. He filled and led all columns on the stats sheet and almost had another triple-double. The Warriors did not want to relent or even extend the series to an all-or-nothing seventh game. Iggy tried his best to get the King to shoot poorly from the floor and did exactly that. LeBron shot only 13 of 33 despite a 32-point performance. Meanwhile, both Iguodala and Curry scored 25 points to start a Warrior rally in the second half. Klay Thompson did not see much action on the floor, not because he played dismally, but because the bench players led by Shaun Livingston really stepped up big. Shaun had 10 points while Klay only had 5. With the Cavs closing in on the Warriors lead in the fourth quarter, the Dubs went back to their bread and butter—the three-point basket—to quell the Cavaliers' rally and to secure the 105-97 win.

With the victory in game six, the Warriors ended the series as the NBA champions. Klay Thompson, Stephen Curry, Andre Iguodala, Draymond Green, and the rest of the Warriors helped the franchise end a long-standing 40-year championship drought in the Bay Area. To the dismay of the Cleveland crowd that wanted LeBron James to win Finals MVP, Andre Iguodala was awarded the award for his tough defense on LeBron and for changing the tide of the series since being inserted into the starting squad. For Klay Thompson who did not perform at his best in the Finals, the most memorable moment was when he was seen hugging coach Steve Kerr who told him, "We did it Klay." Indeed, they had. Klay had become an NBA champion, just like his father. It was a redeeming moment for a man who was not highly recruited as a high school player and who was not a favorite in the NBA Draft. Finally, he and Curry both proved the world wrong by showing us that three-point shooters can indeed win an NBA championship.

Helping the Warriors Break a Record

Basking in the euphoria of an NBA title, Klay Thompson came into the 2015-16 season with much more confidence and a renewed vigor of wanting to win another title, or possibly even more than that. However, the Warriors would suffer a setback. Head coach Steve Kerr underwent surgery to fix a hip problem that had been bothering him. The surgery required him to get a lot of rest and to miss travelling with the team for games. Assistant coach Luke Walton, a two-time champion in his playing years with the Lakers, took over for Kerr on an interim basis. While many thought that Walton could not handle the coaching reigns as well as Kerr did, Luke went on to prove that he had what it took to sit on the big chair. On opening night and on the night that Klay and the Warriors were to receive their NBA championship rings, they blew the New Orleans Pelicans out of Oracle Arena for their first win of the new season. With a much more improved young core led by Curry and Thompson, the Warriors would go on to win game after game that even included a 40-point win against the Grizzlies and two phenomenal performances against bitter rivals the Los Angeles Clippers. Soon after, they were winning games at a record pace. Though the Warriors seemed unbeatable to start the season, Klay Thompson did not perform as well as he did the previous year. He only averaged about 17 points in his first 21 games for the season and did not really have a night where he exploded for a bunch of points. Klay did not score as much overall, maybe because Stephen Curry was scoring almost 10 points more than he did the previous year, or maybe because Thompson did not need to play a lot of minutes and score a lot of points because they were getting wins nevertheless.

Klay Thompson's breakout performance for the early season was his 39-point output against the Indiana Pacers. He shot 10 out 16 from three-point land and, had he played more than the 34 minutes he recorded, he could have tied or broken Kobe Bryant's record for most three-pointers made in a regular season game. Two nights later, Klay followed up that performance by exploding for 43 against the Phoenix Suns in only 30 minutes of action. He scored 27 in the third quarter of that game. There's something about Klay Thompson and third quarters.

With the high output scoring of Stephen Curry and with the steady three-point shooting and defense of Klay Thompson, the Warriors went on to break the record for the most numbers of wins without a loss to start the season. The record was set by the championship Houston Rockets team in 1995. The Warriors would go on to be undefeated until December 12. They had a record of 24-0 heading into Milwaukee. The terrific defense of the Bucks coupled with the steady offense of Greg Monroe helped Milwaukee snap the Warriors' win streak at 24. That streak remains the best undefeated record to start the season in any professional sport in the United States.

In the 27 games that Klay Thompson has played with the Warriors in the 2015-16 season, the Warriors have only lost once and stand at a record of 28-1, which included a Christmas day victory over the Cleveland Cavaliers in their first meeting since battling in the NBA Finals. In only 32 minutes of play, Klay Thompson is averaging 19.3 points, 3.6 rebounds, and 2.4 assists on a career high 46.5 percent shooting from the field and 43.3 percent from three.

Chapter 5: Thompson's Personal Life

Although Klay Thompson was caught being in possession of illegal drugs back in his college years, he has since handled his life as a professional NBA player well, both on and off the court. He never got into any situations he deemed unfavorable for himself. He was often taught valuable life lessons from his father and picked through the brains of other professional athletes as a kid growing up. Klay took all these lessons and implemented them in his daily life.

Klay's father is former NBA player and former top overall draft pick Mychal Thompson. Mychal is of Bohemian descent and has played a total of 14 seasons in the NBA including 12 fruitful years with the Lakers where, together with Magic Johnson and Kareem Abdul-Jabbar, he won two NBA championships. Mychal has always been critical of Klay Thompson's play and remains to be his sons' biggest critic, which helps them to improve their respective games. [xi]Klay's mother is Julie Thompson, who used to play competitive volleyball up until her college years.

He was often considered a quiet and humble guy who had the curiosity of a scientist. Klay would read books in the corner during his childhood, while all the other kids played outside. Thompson is a perfect role model for aspiring athletes looking to take their chances professionally. He has the work ethic and determination to succeed, and for the most part, kept out of trouble. Aside from that one instance that he surely regrets, you won't find Klay in any other mischief. In fact, his parents are trying to teach Klay another lesson in life. With his finances being locked by his parents after a $35,000 suspension was given by the NBA front office, his parents decided to help Klay with long-term financial flexibility. They have him only spending $300 per week for groceries, recreation, etc. and only $3,000 per month on rent. This only adds up to $52, 000 per year, which is a bit unorthodox.[xii] However, this will set up Klay for life when he finds himself with an accumulated wealth. As you can see, his parents play a crucial role in raising Klay the right way. There are just too many professional athletes who have gone broke after making millions of dollars.

Klay Thompson has two other brothers. His older brother is Mychel Thompson, who is also a good basketball player and was formerly playing with the Santa Cruz Warriors, the Golden State Warriors' D-League team. The youngest among the Thompson brothers is Trayce, who plays professionally in the MLB. The Thompson brothers have always been competitive with one another when it came to sports and it was through sports that they were able to find their own identities.

Klay is rumored to be dating Instagram star Hannah Stocking who has 600,000 followers on Vine and close to a million followers on Instagram.

He manages to stay out of trouble, and his parents couldn't be any prouder. He is definitely making a name for himself after having such big shoes to fill.

Look for Klay to continue his path as a true professional athlete for years to come.

Chapter 6: Impact on Basketball

Klay's impact on basketball needs to be addressed in the right fashion. He is a red-hot shooter who can play multiple positions and guard the best of them. With the way he plays, he is a rarity in the NBA. It is not very often that you find a player with such great shooting ability that can guard the best players on the opposing team.

Klay will prove the statistics that suggest that the sons of former NBA players can't make a huge impact in the NBA wrong. It is very rare to witness former NBA player's offspring play at the same level as they did, or taking it to a whole new level entirely. Surprisingly, there are two on one team in Curry and Thompson. They will go down in history as one of the best shooting duos of all time. Both players have more than just a sweet shot in their arsenal; they both have great court vision and playmaking abilities. Curry and Thompson are still very young and have yet to hit their primes, which can be very scary and dangerous for opposing teams.

Thompson will become a huge role model for many young kids and kids of former athletes. He symbolizes that it is possible to create your own destiny, even if your parent's shoes are extremely large and hard to fill. Like his father, Klay has won an NBA championship and has even become an NBA All-Star. His impact on basketball will definitely be a huge one. Many aspiring professional athletes will look at Klay's success and admire his work ethic. He embodies professionalism at its finest and will go down as one of the greatest two guards in history if he keeps up at this pace.

He is one of the best pure shooters in the NBA and managed to make a name for himself on just that one aspect alone. Since then though, Klay has slowly become a more complete player. He has learned how to drive and finish at the basket and has evolved to become a solid perimeter defender. Although he can do much more than just shoot, many will take his journey as a wakeup call to develop the fundamentals in any sport. Klay has mastered the fundamental skills of a shooting guard and has never betrayed his tendency to focus on those fundamentals just to play with flair and style like Kobe and MJ have done. Like with anything however, whether in business, sports, or in school, it is vital to learn the basics first and to truly master them. With hard work and repetition, it is possible to achieve great success by mastering the basics. Although Klay has many more years to come in his NBA career, he has already established himself as a future superstar.

Because of Klay, the shooting guard position has maintained its identity of being able to stretch the floor via the three-pointer. He has continued what three-point specialist shooting guards Reggie Miller, Ray Allen, and Alan Houston have started. He has personified the "shooting" in shooting guard and has been a role model for kids that lack the amount of athleticism and the size that most other NBA superstars have. Although Klay was never very athletic, he has used his fundamental shooting stroke to make his name in the NBA. More important than his shooting, he is a very good decision maker on the court and shows that you don't necessarily have to shot a ton of shots just to be able to score more than 20. Klay has shown that you should just stick to the shots you know you can make, which can help your team win games. His journey through the NBA will be highly documented and praised for his ability to keep his head above water and for his ability to just suddenly explode for consecutive long-ranged baskets. There are many situations that can arise when playing professionally and Klay has managed to keep himself grounded. Parents may also take note from the way he was raised and how his parents continue to play an integral role in his life. His life is by no means perfect, but his journey is definitely one that many kids can aspire to go through themselves.

Chapter 7: Thompson's Legacy and Future

Although it is extremely difficult to predict Klay's legacy in the NBA considering he is still presently playing, Klay will go down as one of the best pure shooters in the game. With the way he has been shooting the ball and with the success of his team, he has the chance to become one of the greatest two guards in NBA history if he keeps improving. Barring any setbacks or any serious injuries, Klay will leave the NBA knowing that he played the best basketball he could ever play in his life and knowing that his abilities have helped his team in winning an NBA Championship.

He may not be as close to Kobe Bryant and Michael Jordan in regards to their legacies or their basketball skills, but he will prove to have a huge impact when he leaves the game just by his ability to shoot the three-pointer alone. With idols like Penny Hardaway, Kobe

Bryant, and Alan Houston to model his game after, Klay definitely chose a great bunch of players to admire. Despite idolizing such players, Klay Thompson's way of playing is more reminiscent of Reggie Miller and Ray Allen in that they are always in constant movement to find screens and open spots on the floor to be able to shoot the ball. He plays the game the way he wants to play it and never backs down from a challenge.

The legacy that he will leave behind will be more about his character, work ethic, and determination. There are not many NBA players who share the same mentality and poise like the greatest to have ever played. Kobe Bryant is known to have one of the best work ethics in NBA history and often over-trained because he did not know when to quit. One night when the Lakers were set to face off against Klay and the Golden State Warriors, Kobe entered the workout area thinking he had the place all to himself. In a pleasant surprise, he found Klay Thompson already in the gym doing a workout himself. This is the kind of work ethic that only great players have, and it is clear that Klay definitely has it. Klay Thompson immediately gleamed when he found out that he got a compliment from one of his idols.

Klay Thompson is the type of player who shoots a lot of three-pointers and makes them at a high percentage. He is your prototypical spot-up shooter. Klay has gone out to say that he does not want to be known simply as such, and has shown flashes of his ability to finish at the basket and even defend at a very high level. With that, Klay has become one of the best two-way wingmen in the league along with guys like Jimmy Butler, Paul George, and Kawhi Leonard. With his ability to shoot the jumper, Klay can suddenly get hot as the sun and seems like his shots cannot miss. He has shown that ability many times, especially when he scored 37 points, which is an NBA record for a single quarter, in the third quarter in a game against the Sacramento Kings. He has also scored 27 points in the third quarter in a recent game against the Phoenix Suns. He is your definition of how hot a microwave oven is supposed to be.

As a Warrior, Klay has become one of the best players in the history of the franchise. That is something to proud of considering that there have been big names in the Warriors' history, such as Wilt Chamberlain, Rick Barry, Tim Hardaway, and Chris Mullin. Klay's numbers may not be seem so gaudy, but his biggest impact as a Warrior is his ability to space the floor and make the right decisions. Of course, not too many Warriors players can go out and say that they were a go-to-guy in a championship team. In the Warriors' title run in 2015, Klay Thompson was Golden State's second leading scorer at about 21 a game behind the 23 of Stephen Curry. And since then, he has always been the second highest scorer on the team because of how he can suddenly get hot and score consecutive baskets.

With how Klay Thompson has shown his importance in the Warriors' championship run and with how he is virtually locked in Golden State with his big contract, expect Klay to maintain his role as one of the go-to-guys in the Warriors team for several more years to come. Together with Stephen Curry, the Splash Brothers have shown and continue to show the world that the three-point shot remains the deadliest weapon in the NBA. Considering that three-point shooting is a fundamentally sound weapon to have, Klay may even play as long as both Reggie Miller and Ray Allen did in the NBA. More importantly, he could very well surpass those two players as the best three-point shooting two guard in the history in NBA since he (and Stephen Curry) is on pace of breaking Ray Allen's record for most three-pointers in a career. As long as he stays healthy and as long as he remains focused on the prize, Klay Thompson will keep on shooting his way up the annals of Warriors and NBA history.

Final Word/About the Author

I was born and raised in Norwalk, Connecticut. Growing up, I could often be found spending many nights watching basketball, soccer, and football matches with my father in the family living room. I love sports and everything that sports can embody. I believe that sports are one of most genuine forms of competition, heart, and determination. I write my works to learn more about influential athletes in the hopes that from my writing, you the reader can walk away inspired to put in an equal if not greater amount of hard work and perseverance to pursue your goals. If you enjoyed *Klay Thompson: The Inspiring Story of One of Basketball's Greatest Sharp Shooter,* please leave a review! Also, you can read more of my works on *Colin Kaepernick, Aaron Rodgers, Peyton Manning, Tom Brady, Russell Wilson, Michael Jordan, LeBron James, Kevin Garnett, Paul George, Kyrie Irving, Stephen Curry, Kevin Durant, Russell Westbrook, Anthony Davis, Chris Paul, Blake Griffin,*

Kobe Bryant, Joakim Noah, Scottie Pippen, Carmelo Anthony, Kevin Love, Grant Hill, Tracy McGrady, Vince Carter, Patrick Ewing, Karl Malone, Tony Parker, Allen Iverson, Hakeem Olajuwon, Reggie Miller, Michael Carter-Williams, John Wall, James Harden, Tim Duncan, and *Steve Nash* in the Kindle Store. If you love basketball, check out my website at claytongeoffreys.com to join my exclusive list where I let you know about my latest books and give you lots of goodies.

Like what you read?

I write because I love sharing the stories of influential people like Klay Thompson with fantastic readers like you. My readers inspire me to write more so please do not hesitate to let me know what you thought by leaving a review! If you love books on life, basketball, or productivity, check out my website at claytongeoffreys.com to join my exclusive list where I let you know about my latest books. Aside from being the first to hear about my latest releases, you can also download a free copy of *33 Life Lessons: Success Principles, Career Advice & Habits of Successful People.* See you there!

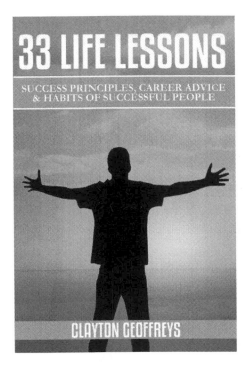

References

[i] Amato, Laura. "Mychal & Julie Thompson, Klay's Parents: 5 Fast Facts You Need to Know". *Heavy.* 4 June 2015. Web

[ii] "Klay Thompson Family Upbringing: The Quiet Kid Played Baseball with Kevin Love Too". *Let's Go Warriors.* Web

[iii] Zarrabi, Nima. "I Changed A Lot." *SLAM Online.* 9 December 2015. Web

[iv] Brown, Daniel. "Klay Thompson's High School Coach Marvels at Transformation". *Mercury News.* Web

[v] "For Golden State Warriors' Klay Thompson, the road to NBA Finals started at Santa Margarita High". *Orange County Register.* 4 June 2015. Web

[vi] "Klay Thompson". *NBA Draft.* Web

[vii] "Klay Thompson". *NBA Draft.* Web

[viii] "Klay Thompson". *Draft Express.* Web

[ix] "Klay Thompson". *NBA Draft.* Web

[x] "Klay Thompson". *NBA Draft.* Web

[xi] Witz, Billy. "Father's Criticism, Amplified". *New York Times.* 21 November 2014. Web

[xii] Witz, Billy. "Father's Criticism, Amplified". *New York Times.* 21 November 2014. Web

Made in the USA
Lexington, KY
08 November 2016